GREAT BIBLE STO

THE STORY OF
JESUS

Adapted by Maxine Nodel   **Illustrated by Norman Nodel**

BARONET BOOKS is a registered trademark of Playmore Inc., Publishers
and Waldman Publishing Corp., New York, N.Y.

Copyright © MCMXCIII Playmore Inc., Publishers
and Waldman Publishing Corp., New York, New York

BARONET BOOKS, NEW YORK, NEW YORK
Printed in China

In Nazareth in the Holy Land, lived a good and pure young woman named Mary. She was engaged to Joseph a local carpenter. One day an angel appeared before her.

"Rejoice," said the angel, "for you are to have a child. You will name him Jesus. This will be the child of God, not the child of your husband."

Mary understood and she and Joseph were married.

Caesar Augustus, the Roman emperor, wanted to find out how many people were living under his rule, so he ordered everyone to return to the place where they had been born.

Joseph came from Bethlehem. He and Mary had many miles to travel.

When they arrived, they knocked at the door of an inn. They were told there was no room and were forced to find shelter in a nearby stable. There Jesus was born.

That night, shepherds in the nearby hills saw a brilliant light in the sky. Suddenly the voice of an angel declared: "Do not be afraid, I have good news. The savior has been born, Christ our Lord. You will find the baby lying in a manger."

The shepherds followed the bright light. They came to the stable where Mary had wrapped the newborn child in swaddling clothes and gently laid him down to rest on the soft hay. The shepherds returned to the hillside to tell others of the great news.

At this time, cruel Herod was king in Jerusalem. Three wise men, following a star, came there to find the newborn king.

These men asked King Herod, "Where is the newborn king? We have come to worship him."

King Herod told the wise men to find the child. They followed the star to the manger.

The wise men bowed to the baby and gave him gifts of gold, frankincense, and myrrh.

When the wise men told King Herod about Jesus, he was jealous of this new king. He ordered that all the children in Bethlehem two years and younger should be killed.

Joseph had a dream in which he was warned of Herod's evil decree. With Mary and Jesus, he escaped to Egypt. They only returned after King Herod died.

When Jesus was twelve, his mother took him to the temple in Jerusalem to celebrate the Passover holiday. The elders were amazed at the answers the young boy gave to their questions, and they marvelled at his wisdom.

Jesus and Mary returned to Nazareth, where Joseph taught him the carpenter's trade. He lived a simple life for eighteen years.
    But Jesus knew he had a great mission in life to fulfill, and that his life would be very different from Joseph's.

John the Baptist was preaching in the wilderness. Jesus went to be baptized and to study with this holy man.

When John saw Jesus, he felt God's presence. "You should baptize me," John told Jesus, "for you are much greater than I."

John knew Jesus was the savior and urged all who listened to repent for their sins, since the savior had come to earth.

Jesus spent forty days and forty nights in the wilderness, thinking about the power God had given him and how to use it wisely.

Satan tempted Jesus, but Jesus resisted him. Jesus wandered through the countryside teaching goodness and God's ways.

When John the Baptist proclaimed Jesus as the savior, twelve of his followers became Jesus's first disciples. They were called the Apostles.

More and more people became followers of Jesus. He healed people of illnesses and performed many miracles. Jesus even raised Lazarus from the dead.

Jesus traveled through the Holy Land, telling stories and parables that taught the way to live a good life.

He preached the Sermon on the Mount, explaining his beliefs in simple ways so all the people could understand.

Jesus went up to Jerusalem for the Passover holiday. As he rode through Jerusalem on a white donkey, palm branches were laid before him.

At the Last Supper, he told
his disciples that before dawn one
of them would betray him.

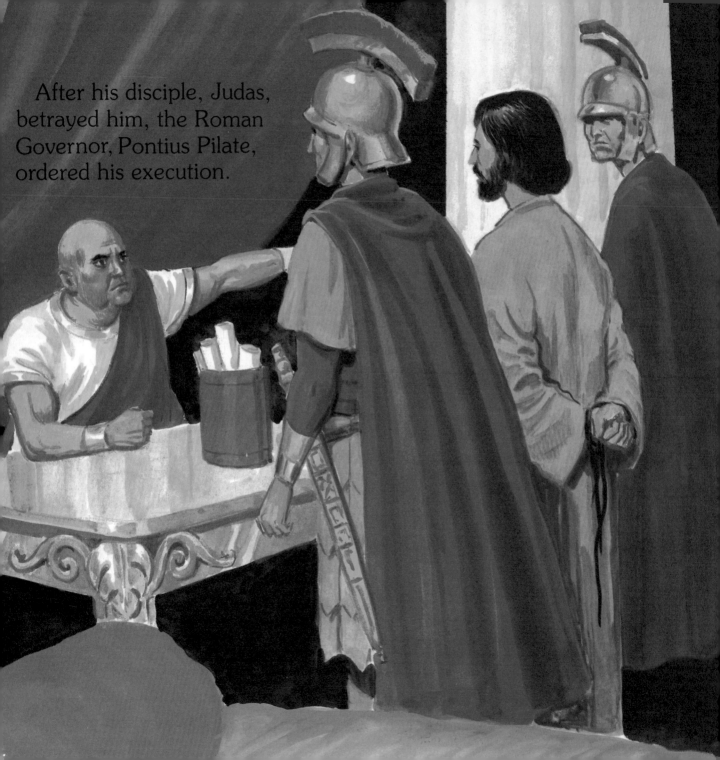

After his disciple, Judas, betrayed him, the Roman Governor, Pontius Pilate, ordered his execution.

He was made to wear a crown of thorns and carry a heavy wooden cross to Mount Calvary, where he was crucified.

On the cross he asked for mercy for man. "Forgive them father, for they know not what they do," he prayed.

After Jesus died, his body was placed in a tomb. The next Sunday, when women came there to annoint his body, the tomb was empty.

Two angels suddenly appeared. "Do not look for the living among the dead," the angels said. "Jesus is not here. He has risen!"